The Lessons of Icarus
And the Pursuit of Happiness

Wm. R. Fowler III

"Alright, we know that you can fly high...
The question is whether or not you can land"[*]

---
[*] Anonymous

Copyright © 2011 by Wm. R. Fowler III
All rights reserved. No parts of this publication may be reproduced, distributed, or transmitted in any form or by any means, including photocopying, recording, or other electronic or mechanical methods, without prior written permission from the publisher, except in the case of brief quotations embodied in critical reviews and certain other noncommercial uses permitted by copyright law. For permission requests, write to the publisher, addressed "Attn: Permission Requests", at the following email address: TLOI.Contact@gmail.com

Ordering Information
This book is available in special quantity discounts when ordered directly from the publisher. For details please send an inquiry to the following email address: TLOI.Contact@gmail.com, labeled "Attn: Special Sales Requests"

www.thelessonsoficarus.com

All we have is here and now
All our lives, out there to find

Joe Cocker

Forward:

How does the mythical Icarus relate to this book?

The 'real' Icarus flew amazingly high in his imagination...

In a flash of insight he acquired an understanding of the dynamics that alter reality... and then 'played' with them.

Icarus was driven insane by the enormity of the results of this behavior.

I am Icarus.

I had learned the secrets of actualization but not the wisdom to apply them strategically. The 5 'lessons' themselves come from brutal experience and years of critical examination. *The 5 'lessons' are simply the rules of the game.*

"The Lessons of Icarus" is a combination of the secrets of creation along with the often overlooked wisdom to use them safely.

Why the emphasis on anxiety? Is this a book about anxiety?

Anxiety is shown as a foundation for the other concepts to stand upon.

Anxiety is the price we must pay for seeking our fullest 'potential' in life. We need to understand it, and learn how to manage it because *it is the only meaningful measure of our limitations*...

How did this book come into existence?

The 'existence' of this book is a quintessential example of 'the philosophy' *applied*... This book did not create itself. It was, at one point, simply a desirable possibility...

If you had to sum up the purpose of this book?

To share the "How To" for the *process* of complete and total Self-Empowerment…

A timely and powerful perspective in our collective search for meaning.

Preface:

May you never come to an understanding that you aren't prepared for...

***

As I pull out and light yet one more cigarette, I am reminded of what it really means to be addicted to mind altering chemicals. I am not pleased about my own addictions.

Many people have trouble understanding how a reasonable person can make such chronically stupid and unreasonable decisions.

I will state it simply and clearly, but the next three statements create a circular loop in logic:

A) A smoker (alcoholic, meth freak, etc.) has developed a *personal reality* where such behavior is considered acceptable.

B) Each of us must accept ourselves. This is a minimal requirement to survival.

C) Go to A)

It is simple:

Decisions direct behavior and behavior affects reality.

***

This is why people may need to hit 'rock bottom' before they decide to change the way they look at their lives. Their realities are crashing so hard against everyone else's that they have become completely dysfunctional.

And when we make statements like 'how people look at life', don't we really mean how people perceive reality itself? Isn't the whole point with an addict that he/she has stopped accepting unpleasant truths? Has stopped growing, etc.?

The *functional* contrast is seen whenever an individual's reality significantly deviates from what we could call mutual or 'Collective Reality'. The greater the contrast the greater the difficulties an individual will experience in achieving desired end results.

Examples of deviating behaviors result from all of our possible traits: sociability, lethargy, hygiene, intelligence, ethics, etc.

But each of our lives is unique, and our experiences add diversity to the cultures that we live in. Diversity, as always, introduces the 'new'…

We grow and learn our lessons and then share them with our families and others…

It is with such thoughts that this discussion has been created…

This book was written to get the attention of people who want 'more' out of Life: People seeking harmony, achievement, and most importantly a sense of meaning in their lives…

Do you feel that your life is consistent with the mouse in the little wheel?

What happened to your freedom?

Would you be willing to **work** to get it back?

The following discussion explains *why* and *how* you can change your expectations in life to achieve a "Rock High" instead of a "Rock Bottom".

The lessons and the underlying philosophy are based on the real world and real world experiences.

Some parts of the message are not new… simply approached from a new perspective. This is an *assimilation* of various diverse facts and documented phenomena. In the end, it should all tie together as a fulfilling, exciting, internally consistent, and self-supporting way of life.

To truly understand this point of view you must put the pieces together by yourself: This book represents a 'puzzle'. All of the pieces of this puzzle have been carefully laid out for you.

But what is the point of this discussion?

As a fact, this philosophy is intended to provide you 'the path' to your **own definition** of happiness.

If you allow it… this perspective will provide you with a truly profound approach to the "Pursuit of Happiness" itself…

***

The fundamental issue that this discussion addresses is the concept of Destiny. In other words, is there a 'purpose' woven into the complexities of our lives?

Is there a basic meaning to Life that we can actually feel and appreciate?

Does Destiny actually exist? Or are we simply 'reacting' to the often complex situations that we find ourselves in?

The purpose of this discussion is to convince you that Destiny **does** exist… *but so does simple Fate.*

***

Fate defined: an 'unexamined' Destiny

***

The distinction is based only on 'intention'...

There are remarkable truths in the existence that we share. I ask that you be patient and open mindedly consider the points along this short 'stroll'. The following lessons and truths have been hard won in this sometimes baffling thing called 'Reality'. If you understand the simple message of this philosophy then you will indeed learn how to direct your own Destiny...

The source of our Destinies is carefully hidden in plain view

The level of effort you spend in understanding this philosophy will proportionally improve the level of control that you have *on the future*...

Every attempt has been made to work within the framework of accepted science and philosophy. The statements and conclusions within this discussion are presumed to be 'self-evident' upon study and reflection.

Table of Contents:

1) Introduction:
   The Truth about Anxiety

   1: Making Decisions   1
   2: Living in the NOW   9
   3: The Fall of Icarus   15

2) Challenge:
   The Truth about Reality

   1: Medicine Defines 'Predisposition'   17
   2: Icarus, washed upon the beach,
       struggles to stand   21
   3: Chaos Theory   27
   4: The Double Blind Test   29
   5: The Observer Effect   31

3) Cause and Effect:
   The Truth about the Power of Choice

   1: What Do You Want?   39
   2: Oxymoron: Meaningful Coincidence   45

Conclusion   47

References   54

1) Introduction:
The Truth about Anxiety

1: Making Decisions

Daedalus fashioned two pairs of wings out of wax and feathers for himself and his son [Icarus]. Before they took off from the island, Daedalus warned his son not to fly too close to the sun, nor too close to the sea. Overcome by the giddiness that flying lent him, Icarus soared through the sky curiously, but in the process he came too close to the sun, which melted the wax. Icarus kept flapping his wings but soon realized that he had no feathers left and that he was only flapping his bare arms. And so, Icarus fell into the sea...

My life had gradually descended into a living hell.

I had become so successful at altering my environmental influences that I was no longer in control of them. My environment, and the influence it exerted, had grown so huge that it had taken on a life of its own...

It seemed that my every gesture, every utterance, was reflected immediately in the behavior of others. The entire world was a hall of mirrors and I was at its very center...

My life was a fishbowl, and I was being poked and prodded by people who I didn't know or understand. For a period of time, I was at the very center of *all attention*.

I am not asking for you to understand or believe...

But it is too easy to explain such events as the 'mere perceptions' of a troubled mind. There is a basic question of cause and effect... Chicken and egg.

The truth is that mental illness is little understood by those who have never experienced it.

Here is the point: Life *continues* despite the fact that there are troubling thoughts going through a person's mind…

The effect is that a person's judgment is profoundly altered by these troubling thoughts. He will make **bad decisions**… And hopefully, before it is too late, seek help.

This is the part that most people don't appreciate: The first goal is getting your mind back on solid ground. The second, and far more difficult part, is fixing the problems in your life that are the results of your poor decisions (*and* addressing the actual cause and nature of the illness itself).

This is made all the more difficult because after such a mental breakdown there will be a new 'label' applied to you: The label of having lost one's mind…

It is completely natural to fear and avoid this label…

You would find that it's not enough that the mind has come back in the meantime. Try to imagine awakening from such a state of confusion. There may be little you can clearly remember. But it actually happened: You clinically "lost it".

Everyone has the potential for losing their grip on things when experiencing sufficient stress and anxiety.

It is no wonder that people are conservative about making decisions that affect their lives. Change is stressful and can cause a great deal of anxiety. Stress and anxiety, when pushed to the breaking point, are not only extremely unpleasant but will cause a human mind to begin to break apart…

This is *not* inevitable and there are many things you can do to prevent it. From someone who has experienced 'mind breaking' anxiety… I can assure you that the only solution is *courage* in the face of fear.

We must have *faith* that things will work out for the best.

This is not an option. This is a *requirement* for happiness. Hopelessness and unfocused fear are indeed *signs of mental illness*...

The worst aspects of my own mental illness are managed through medications. I have Bipolar Disorder, so I can feel depths of depression at times but also the opposite: Mania is the opposite of depression. It is known for its hyperactivity, poor judgment, and endless energy.

Some people actually enjoy this energy, and so stop taking their medications. The resulting poor judgment and activities predictably destroys their lives.

So we have the two 'poles' of Bipolar Disorder: Down and depressed or manic and 'crazy'...

It is better to simply face mental illness for what it is NOT... We tend to focus on treating the illness with therapy and medications. We should, instead, set a **priority** for '<u>**Mental Wellness**</u>'.

Between the two extremes of Bipolar Disorder is a *third state of mind:* Hypomania. People who can maintain a 'hypo manic' (below manic) state of mind are *wildly* successful in life.

These are the fortunate few. Energy, creativity, productivity, achievement, and the experience of having an impact on their world cause a sense of 'purpose' in their lives. Leaders, Artists, and Captains of Industry... People who have faced their fears, and see few meaningful limitations...

This is a *desirable* state of mind.

But our 'state of mind' can change with the situation at hand if we are not careful. We must learn to stop simply 'reacting' to events. Just as we fight to maintain our sanity... we should fight to maintain a ***desirable state of mind.***

This is especially difficult to do if you suffer from *any underlying or latent form* of mental illness. Mental illness can be described as 'a *persistently unhealthy* state of mind'.

With my own mental illness I have experienced many states of mind, and I can assure you that *some are better than others…*

The process of achieving and maintaining a desirable state of mind is what this book was 'designed' to convey.

***

Many will say that this little book is 'fragmented', meaning without apparent structure. This is all too true.

But this is not a novel; this is a pathway to happiness. If the pieces don't seem to fit together at first please be patient. It is at the moment when you start to 'see' your future that you will understand the purpose of this discussion… And it will change the way that you look at your life.

You will understand that fear and anxiety are also states of mind… and can be easily overcome through practice and understanding.

So we begin…

***

We all know what happens when we use the wrong tool to fix a problem: The problem remains or gets worse and we may even have damaged the tool. Balance in life requires the use of the right tools at the right times. We must not lose our perspective: We must maintain control of our perceptions…

Fortunately experience trains us how to react to the harsher realities that are presented to us. Have you ever been fired from a job? Dropped by a lover? Failed, in some way, to do something that seemed a sure thing?

Have you ever had an 'undesirable outcome?'

It is not the crisis but your reaction to it that matters... Even more important is the fact that you should have foreseen the possibility and should have had contingency plans in place.

This is a certainty because you created the undesired outcome. You are at least partially responsible that things didn't work out in the first place…

It is completely natural to resist this idea, as we will see. However, it is crucial that we understand and accept Reality for what it is:

The simple truth is that you are an active player in your own future whether you believe it or not.

***

It is, of course, dangerous to assert a 'simple truth' outside of any specific context. It is the context, and the perspective that defines what is true or even what is 'real'.

Most people believe that reality is a safe and stable idea. After all, it is simply all that there is and all that happens.

Yet we recognize with the simplicity of a car's dirty windshield that our *perception* of reality can be quite different from that of person walking his dog on the *same sunny day*…

Philosophers have struggled with the definition of what is real throughout history. Many have come to unexpected conclusions.

For our purposes we will adopt, as a starting point, a branch of thinking known as Existentialism:

> *"We accept the reality of the world with which we're presented"*[*]

Existentialism focuses on the perspective of the individual as he struggles to find *meaning* in a world that can seem inherently devoid of it...

"Existential philosophy is the "explicit conceptual manifestation of an existential attitude"[1] that begins with a sense of disorientation and confusion in the face of an apparently meaningless or absurd world." [2,3]

To put it more practically this could describe us as small children, newborn to the world. We start as blank sheets to be written upon. What we observe and what we are told begins the process of creating ever expanding sets of meaningful realities for the rest of our lives. Collectively, these meaningful realities make up our perceptions of our own sense of 'existence'.

Typical influences that provide meaning to life include religion, values, and any influences caused by our own desires...

We accept what we observe to be true.

We accept what we are told to be true.

*We rarely dare challenge what we **believe to be real**...*

An example: Elephants are trained at a young age that they cannot break the ropes that are holding them in place. The ropes are exceptionally strong: Unbreakable for an infant elephant. As the elephant grows larger, the rope grows smaller until it is basically just a piece of string.

---

[*]Christof, main character of the 1998 *Truman Show*, a film directed by and written by Andrew Niccol

The elephant 'knows' that it is impossible to break.

More important to our discussion, however, is the fact that the continuing existence of the string represents a significant portion of 'Reality' for the elephant... The 'rope' has been the one constant in the elephant's entire life...

Let's just think about that...Why doesn't the elephant try to break that piece of string to gain his freedom? *Why do we* tend choose the familiar, safe path?

Existential philosophy explains this type of mental block as 'angst', or anxiety. The fundamental nature of anxiety is shown to be a side effect of *freedom itself*...

"Angst, sometimes called dread, anxiety or even anguish is a term that is common to many existentialist thinkers. It is generally held to be the experience of our freedom and responsibility. The archetypal example is the experience one has when standing on a cliff where one not only fears falling off it, but also dreads the possibility of throwing oneself off. In this experience that "nothing is holding me back", one senses the lack of anything that predetermines you to either throw yourself off or to stand still, and one experiences one's own freedom." [4]

And just like when you imagine looking down that dangerous cliff's edge, you will naturally feel increasing anxiety as you even *approach the thought* of using your freedom to make a real change in your life. **This represents your own 'strings attached', just like the poor elephant...**

***

It is such unfocussed anxiety over consequences that prevents people from committing to a new direction in life.

We should label this increasing anxiety effect a 'self limiting function' that continually draws us back so our comfortable reality whenever we contemplate using freedom to change our lives...

Ironically, we cannot escape ultimate responsibility by simply refusing to acknowledge it. Our *individual* results are the totality of our current realities... **our lives, our happiness itself.** *We make the choices... and then we must live with them.*

Each of us must find our *own* sense of meaning in life... The fact that many blame others or situational factors is 'unfortunate'.

We *must* accept the fact that we are responsible for the outcomes of our decisions.

"With complete freedom to decide, and complete responsibility for the outcome of decisions, comes anxiety (angst). Anxiety's importance in existentialism makes it a popular topic in psychotherapy. Therapists often use existential philosophy to explain the patient's anxiety. Psychotherapists using an existential approach believe that a patient can harness his anxiety and use it constructively. Instead of suppressing anxiety, patients are advised to use it as grounds for change. By embracing anxiety as inevitable, a person can use it to achieve his full potential in life."[5]

It is always a good exercise to look back on some of our disappointments and ask if things would have been different had we accepted more responsibility at the time...

* * *

Total acceptance of responsibility for those things that we can control and the *potential* anxiety that goes along with it is the price that must be paid in order to successfully implement the lessons of this discussion.

2: Living in the NOW

Even the highest levels of awareness will require time to experiment and observe in order to understand how things work in an unknown environment. We need to remember, however, that it is our ability to consistently achieve higher levels of awareness that separates us from all other known forms of life...

We know that we are somehow unique in the world, and it is this uniqueness that defines us as humans.

But what is the most fundamental way of describing this uniqueness?

What talent must have existed in humankind *before* we learned to create fire, the wheel, and language?

The special talent is our ability to effortlessly perceive beyond the world of the NOW. This includes *all abstract thought* but we will focus on the perception of the passage of time.

It will help to view things from the elephant's perspective again: An elephant, like us, can feel and will react to threatening situations. The resulting adrenaline rush, stress, and immediate increase in awareness will occur at any threatening moment. This is known as the "Fight or Flight" reaction. It happens in the NOW. People feel it very clearly at moments when we *almost* have a car accident. Heart pumping, rapid breath. This is an animal reaction but we are still bound by its reality. It is as natural for us as it is for the elephant and the dog and the bird... This is what we usually refer to as 'stress'.

The NOW can be described as the current instant in time and space. It is continually changing but it requires human level awareness in order to perceive that changes are occurring **at all**. An animal's perception is strictly bound within the NOW.

✡ Birds don't **worry** about what might happen in the **future**. Cows never feel **guilty** about things they have done in the **past**... These burdens fall only on human shoulders, and we know deep down in our hearts that we can be <u>overwhelmed by the resulting anxiety</u>...

***

We need to remember that animals cannot perceive the flow of time and this is WHY animals cannot feel *Anxiety*...

But our effortless ability to perceive the 'before and after' can never be based on perfect information. Different people, with different backgrounds, will have entirely different perspectives on the same event as it occurs through time…

Expectations for the future will be even more diverse among individuals.

The more unclear the perceived causal factors and their impact on actual results the more anxiety we tend to feel: We feel less 'in control' when we don't understand the factors that are driving events forward. Therefore it is a natural trait for people to spend effort trying to get 'ever better' information on the environmental factors that combine to create change.

***

To deal with the anxiety we can do well to remember that we *can act like an animal acts.* Animals don't feel any stress when they are not being threatened. Are you feeling threatened right now? If so, is it something that *might* happen in the future? Do you ever get a sense of unease because you have made mistakes before?

A simple suggestion is to devote one half hour each day to feeling 'like a cow chewing his cud'. No stress, just a full acceptance that things **are the way that they are**. Like an animal: *Alertness without anxiety*. Give yourself some down time. Recharge your sense of humor.

We need to find this time to live in the NOW in order to be as naturally anxiety free as the animals are. This time will reduce both your anxiety and stress levels.

In fact, you can use this technique whenever anxiety threatens to become overwhelming: Simply close your eyes and **practice** detaching from your current stream of thoughts. Snap back into phase with the NOW. See how long you can exercise your focus on this one single instance of infinity…

***

Now that we have established a good starting point, it is time to clarify a few more things about two very similar but distinct concepts:

We need to more clearly define the terms 'anxiety' and 'stress' as they relate to your happiness.

Stress is a reaction to a specific perceived threat. Your imagination will offer many options for how to respond to this threat. It occurs within the snapshots of the NOW.

Anxiety is a reaction to a perceived but unknown or unspecified threat. There will be no way to prepare because it is 'undefined'. There are no clear solutions. There are no definable plans. It is not associated to any specific time, so it is felt at all times. The resultant emotion is fear… It is 'irrational'.

Even with our time traveling perceptions, *stress* is a natural and healthy part of life. It is resolved by fixing the problem, making a plan (i.e. "mental time travel") ... or exercise, or meditation.

Anxiety is an entirely different issue, and a dangerous one at that. Remember, however, that the Existentialists associate Freedom with anxiety. What can we do about this thing?

We need to remember that anxiety cannot exist in the NOW. If you can detach yourself for a moment and come into 'phase' with your current surroundings you will quickly understand that anxiety is based upon *perception alone*. If you can learn to live in the NOW then *there is no anxiety. It simply cannot exist...*

So what does anxiety **really represent?**

The clearest answer might be that it represents fear of both the unknown and the unknowable. The simplest way to accept it is to consider it to be 'the big random variable in life'. It might be considered the 'rolling of the dice'. If you decide to take a chance in life it is because you are willing to risk it... *knowing that you cannot know the future...*

In any case, we can all do well to remember:

***

"Fear is the lock and laughter the key to your heart" [*]

***

Throwing caution to the wind and taking big risks is the 'simple way'. There is another way of addressing the unknown that is simple, effective, and ensures a startling sense of 'purpose' to

---

[*] Crosby Stills & Nash 1969 'Sweet Judy Blue Eyes'

your life. What you will see occurring as we progress through this discussion will be examples of how Reality is in fact a *very unstable circumstance.*

You will be shown through concepts that are widely accepted that Reality is more like a *matrix / flux of dynamic energies and patterns constantly upstanding each other in a never ending battle for actualization: A crashing standing wave of 'NOW'...*

We all play this same game according to the various levels of awareness that we have of it. However, we cannot escape the results by denying our own roles in the process.

Your fate is laid out before you… It will remain unchanged unless you change it...

This leads to the first 'How To' Lesson of Icarus:

***

You must choose to work within the flow of time. Stand in the way of events at your own peril...

***

Instead, create your own events in time. This is something you can control and it costs you nothing.

In the end you will understand that we are discussing a *personal mastery of how reality self-actualizes.*

***

"Does the man make the journey, or does the journey make the man?"*

***

---
* *'A Voyage Beyond Reason'*, by Tom Gauthier

3: The Fall of Icarus

The following is an excerpt from an original, unpublished version of this book, after my first true attempt to change reality...

My anxiety level was through the roof. I felt like I was going to completely fly apart...

I finally saw a Psychiatrist and he immediately gave me a diagnosis: Depressive Anxiety. He prescribed an old favorite mix called Triavil. I had told him that I was 'running around faster and faster within a box that was growing smaller'. I wasn't eating or sleeping.

From the Existentialist's view:

"Man exists in a state of distance from the world that he nonetheless remains in the midst of. This distance is what enables man to project meaning into the disinterested world ... This projected meaning remains fragile, constantly facing breakdown for any reason — from a tragedy to a particularly insightful moment. In such a breakdown, we are put face to face with the naked meaninglessness of the world, and the results can be devastating."[6]

And so Icarus fell into the sea...

As smart and confident as I had been that I could change the course of events, I felt that all I really had done was 'interfere'... and cause a big mess for a lot of people.

Looking back, it was the medically induced stupor that had successfully terminated my manic episode. It took about one year to find balance in life again.

But somehow I felt injured, as if disabled in some indefinable way.

In fact *I was injured*, for unbounded anxiety had 'burned a hole' in my imagination that could lead to the edge of madness. *It is very difficult to explain the anxiety that comes from being let down by your own mind...*

Further, with each episode of my disorder comes an increase in the likelihood of another episode. One becomes two, two becomes four, etc.

I didn't know any of this at the time. I had no idea what was wrong with me.

It was to be another seven years before I was correctly diagnosed. All I planned at the time was that if I ever got into that kind of heat again, I would stand through it and *survive*. I would make wings designed to withstand that searing heat... I would develop a *strategy*.

I knew that Icarus would fly again...

2: Challenge:
The Truth about Reality

1: Medicine Defines 'Predisposition'

Most of us never experience serious problems associated with freedom and the anxiety that comes along with it. However, most of us never dare challenge our assumptions about Reality. Further, most of us never become truly '*invested*' in our own Destinies.

This issue is especially important to people who have potential medical problems that can be 'triggered' by serious anxiety. There are many serious medical issues that can be brought on by anxiety. But this is only *one* of the reasons why we need to examine anxiety so closely...

There are lots of 'triggers' that can create a whole host of medical problems.

The interesting question regards whether or not a person already has such a disease

...before it actually occurs...

Does a medical problem *exist* before it gets triggered? Is it *REAL?*

Interestingly, Medicine answers this question is in a very straightforward manner. The solution is a simple definition: Yes, such a disease exists as a potentiality and it is labeled a 'predisposition'. In many cases it is associated with genetics and is labeled a 'genetic predisposition'.

A dictionary definition of potentiality is: "A latent capacity for becoming or developing."

We have all heard people say things like 'Heart Disease runs in my family'.

There are many accepted examples of such potentialities: diabetes, male pattern baldness, arthritis, etc. They may or may not be 'triggered'...

So, strangely, we are saying that a medical condition can *exist before it actually occurs*...

***

There is a major problem here regarding our 'normal' assumptions about Reality: the very concept of <u>potentiality</u> reveals **'patterns in the future'** *that <u>may or may not</u> be 'triggered' by specific events...*

***

Many potentialities can be influenced by our decisions. Another interesting point is that the concept of predispositions can be applied to any type of reality, not just one's health.

Example: If a student studies for a test he is predisposed to getting a good grade. Of course, he must study the correct materials...he must not show up late, he had better have something to write with, etc.

We accept the fact that uncounted potential outcomes can become very real...

This may seem obvious, but it is our first and easiest **proof** that ***Reality is not what it appears to be***. In fact it is quite amazing: ***There is, at any point in time, an <u>infinite</u> number of potential realities that exist in your future...***

Ask yourself if there are some amazing and wonderful potentialities among the uncounted choices available to you.

Ask yourself if there's a limit to the number of them...

***

If you could only push the ***right 'triggers'...***

If you could only cut the ***right strings...***

2: Icarus, washed upon the beach, struggles to stand (excerpt)

When I started taking the Triavil I slept for three solid days. I finally woke up on a Monday and I had my second appointment with the Psychiatrist.

For the first time in several months I actually felt rested, if somewhat subdued. When I met with the Doctor I remember telling him that 'I can feel my mind trying to jump back into that circular reasoning that was driving me crazy'.

He told me that the medicine made such thinking impossible and I said, "What a relief!". Triavil turned out to be a pretty good medication for terminating my undiagnosed "mood disorder" episode.

There were drawbacks...

I not only felt 'slower', I felt less 'aware' of the circumstances that were surrounding me. My wife said that it turned me into a 'zombie' for the six months that I took it. On hindsight this was exactly what I needed at the time, so I am grateful for Triavil as a short term solution.

Once I stopped taking it, though, I had no protection from further manic episodes. I didn't have that kind of medicine. I had been misdiagnosed, so I didn't really understand about the 'potentiality' for future outbreaks.

What I did come to realize was something I had never considered: awareness itself exists in a million shades of grey: the lower boundary is a coma, and there *is no upper boundary*...

I am not talking about the limits of an animal's awareness (stuck in the NOW), but human awareness among various individuals at different times.

The term 'awareness' can be a very difficult thing to define. It might best be compared to a 'wavelength' or a level of perception.

You might think of a mouse seeing a cat as being suddenly, extremely aware...

Because our bodies cannot distinguish whether threats are real or imagined, our own levels of awareness are stimulated by either stress or anxiety.

After a mentally challenging day, many will purposely limit their awareness in various ways, from distracting themselves with music or gardening to taking drugs or alcohol.

And why do we do such things? Of course, it is simple anxiety… It is *truly essential* to understand the subtle impact that it can have on our lives. It is insidious. It is irrational. Anxiety is the 'enemy' of happiness.

Anxiety is the only thing holding **YOU** back from the life that you really want…

As our levels of awareness increase to the point that we can (intentionally) create our own reality, anxiety can grow like a twisted parasite on our minds.

We need to remember that anxiety is just an emotion. And, like other emotions it can be overcome by our desires, logic, training, and practice.

***

Awareness itself is generally increased by any form of mental stimulation. Human levels of awareness can soar 'higher than the eagles'. If your level of mental awareness rises high enough, you will start to 'see' the future with senses that you develop through practice.

If you doubt this, consider historical examples such as Leonardo da Vinci, Gandhi … Einstein.

Alternatively, awareness can also wallow in the shallows when we have a boring job, a boring friend, a boring life… If you choose this path then you will live a safe and boring existence.

You are free to choose it and you are welcome to the world of *mediocrity.*

But if you want to live for the 'pursuit of happiness', you must develop your own values and principles to guide your steps.

The process of self-actualization that we are discussing will draw deep lines in your 'character'.

Self-Actualization means maximizing the realization and fulfillment of one's human *potential*. (i.e. *potential*ity) ✡

But how can you increase your awareness without increasing your anxiety?

For me, recovering from the craziness of mania, mediocrity sounded pretty good. I chose to pursue it indefinitely. Unfortunately, I had learned to be afraid of the consequences of my own mind's activities…

***

There is a reason that this discussion requires your full attention:

Your mind needs to be 'fully aware' when the moment comes that you truly understand the simple message and *purpose* of this discussion… Though referenced in every section, you will either 'get it' or you will not…

The purpose of this discussion is to explain both why and how to achieve *and* <u>maintain</u> a 'desirable' state of mind…

To achieve this aim, we are reviewing weaknesses and patterns in the fabric of the REAL…

These patterns, when understood and manipulated, allow for the process of changing your world in whatever way is <u>meaningful</u> to <u>you</u>. This provides 'meaning' to your life… and is *the source* of your potential Happiness.

***

A diamond cutter looks closely at the crystal structure of a small rough stone.

With his tools and experience he strikes the stone in just the right way and voila, he reveals the underlying pattern by removing everything else. We see the beautiful diamond that was *already there* inside the rough stone.

***

Cutting the diamond with confidence is perhaps the best metaphor relating to how you can create the world of your own desires. Like the perfect diamond that potentially exists in the rough stone, the future that you **pursue potentially exists in reality. You simply need to** *reveal it to yourself.*

***

This leads us to an important principle that you must follow in order to avoid failure: *Only tell your most trusted the details of what you are in the process of achieving...*

To tell others about your most powerful desires will 'bounce the ball onto their side of the court'. It gives them a chance to take control. Let's discuss why this is dangerous...

Since other people cannot share the strength of your desires, they have no reason to support your goals. No doubt others will have their own desires. They generally don't care about yours.

Another person may truly believe that your desires are foolish or even inappropriate. Perhaps others will think you are trying to rise above your 'station' in life.

Someone might believe that your goals are unrealistic, and try to 'help you' by talking you into something else.

Even worse, others might conclude that your goals are not consistent with theirs. In this case they will actively try to oppose you.

I broke this rule during my first real attempt to intentionally alter my Reality. Perhaps if I had kept my mouth shut I could have achieved what I wanted: To help everyone at the same time.

They say 'No guts, no glory'. Well, there is nothing glorious to others about chipping away at the diamond...about reaching for your desires. *A smart diamond cutter never shows a work in progress...*

***

You can reveal the reality of your achievements once you have revealed the reality to yourself... NOT before...

This is the second Lesson of Icarus

***

The topics in the next three **short** sections discuss specific scientific observations.

It may (at first) be unclear as to how these observations impact the overall discussion…

However, the next three sections lay a foundation upon which we can describe the shockingly simple nature of our <u>'potential'</u> to <u>alter Reality</u>.

3: Chaos Theory

A relatively new subset of Mathematics called Chaos Theory attempts to explain observed tendencies in the structure of nature that address the concept of underlying 'design'. While we will look at a few examples of this counter-intuitive mathematics and discuss some aspects of chaos on a very high level, an in depth study of this type of math is beyond the scope of this discussion.

Basically, Chaos Theory describes underlying patterns in Nature that were once simply assumed to be random. This type of math is not to be confused with the idea of 'chaos' meaning 'out of control'.

A simple example of a chaotic pattern: The location on a tree where a new branch will grow is not random. Randomness would create an occasional branch that is directly above another, overshadowing the lower branch. This would be inefficient. Likewise, there would be open spaces on the trunk that *should* have a branch in order to make the most of the available sunlight.

Most trees are sufficiently complex that we cannot predict exactly where the next branch will grow, but we can predict with some accuracy the boundaries that most of the limbs will reside in. This is why no two trees have the same exact structure yet they all 'look the same' in a general sense.

Tree branches *tend* to grow in places that achieve the greatest efficiency, *given the location of the other existing branches*. Snowflakes, veins and arteries, and many other things share this same tendency where they may all generally 'look the same', but in fact each one is unique. In chaos theory, this concept is referred to as "self-similarity".

Another good example of a chaotic pattern is the weather. Even with our best super-computers we cannot accurately predict the weather for more than a few days out. In fact it is safe to say that we will never be able to truly predict the weather. However, on any given day we can observe that there is clearly a pattern built into the process.

Much effort has been used to try to predict the Stock Markets as well...

Such complex, dynamic systems are said to be 'deterministic', meaning that they have inevitable outcomes (assuming no outside influences). *The outcomes **will not be predictable***, but they are determined by the initial state that the system begins with.

Next week's weather *will* have a pattern to it, though we don't know what that specific pattern will be...

There at least are two important reasons to review these ideas within the context of this discussion:

Once again we can see patterns in the fabric of reality. Nature is hard wired with chaos from the expansion of a flower's petals to the arc of a lightening bolt.

We can become sensitized to the dynamics of such patterns in order to apply our efforts at the best possible moments to affect a desired outcome. It is a truth that 'timing is everything'.

Also, it demonstrates with certainty that absolutely no-one can predict the future with absolute accuracy. When it comes to the combined efforts of people, we all play our own roles in how reality will actualize.

Nature doesn't care if your desired future comes to reality. To Nature one reality is as good as another, especially when we bring human intentions into the equation...

4: The Double Blind Test

The creation of what's known as a double blind test did not come easily to scientists. In fact, it was only after undeniable and repeated failures that scientists accepted the fact that double blind tests were often required when studying people...

In medicine, a blind test is designed so that the people receiving a new test medicine don't know if theirs is the test medicine or a 'sugar pill'. This makes sense if you are familiar with the 'Placebo Effect'. It had been shown that if a person believes that he is receiving a new 'wonder drug' he will benefit from that belief. If the patient believes that a medicine will help him then it will help him (this has been proven time and again). We will refer back to this phenomenon later on.

But the goal of any experiment is to ascertain the independent effects of whatever is being tested. Therefore, since the placebo effect was altering the outcomes of the experiments, it became a requirement that the patients could not know whether they were receiving the new test medicine or a placebo (i.e. 'sugar pill').

Scientists accepted this... However, it later became clear that even the blind test was not sufficient. It was proven that even if the experimenters knew which patients were receiving the real medication the outcomes of experiments were similarly altered.

Begrudgingly, the scientists accepted this fact as well. The solution was to ensure that neither the patients nor the scientists could know which patients were receiving the test medication vs. the placebo.

This is the idea behind a 'double' blind test. Finally, they had a test format where the mere *expectations of outcomes* could not alter the results of the experiments...

Here we see an important weakness in the fabric of reality... The placebo effect has a large role to play in altering your Destiny. You can expect anything you want, and nature will tend to provide it for you. The only requirement is that you must *believe* it can *actually happen.*

5: The Observer Effect

As with Chaos Theory and Double Blind tests, the Observer Effect has profound implications for this discussion. Again, however, we will only discuss an overview of the subject as it relates to our purpose...

The observer effect was most notably formulated in the scientific realm of quantum mechanics. This is a study of how reality behaves on an infinitesimally small scale: At the level of atoms, electrons, etc.

One of the basic laws of quantum mechanics is that particles can exist in simultaneous states: often referred to as 'super-positions'.

One amazing fact is the basic quantum law that says that any attempt to measure the state of a super-position causes it to become one state or another. The particle 'resolves' or 'collapses' into one state simply by being *observed*.

This is a very difficult thing to believe.

It is referred to as the 'Observer Effect'.

There are other definitions of the Observer Effect that better relate to our world. *All contain the same basic concept* that the **measurement or observation** of events can actually **alter** the outcomes of the events.

A simple example is the measurement of electric voltage with a voltmeter. In order to measure the voltage of a circuit the voltmeter must become part of the circuit... and this affects the circuit's voltage.

Another even more intuitive example of the Observer Effect is the way that people's behavior changes when they believe they may be observed by others. We spend enormous amounts of time and resources on 'appearances'. We don't run red lights if there is a police car at the intersection. Authoritarian governments spy on their own people, knowing that it keeps them intimidated and 'in line'.

Notice that when we think about our behavior in front of other people we are reacting to both internal and environmental <u>expectations</u>.

It is truly shocking to realize the pervasiveness of the Observer Effect on our lives... Much of what we do is driven by our perceived expectations from ***others...*** as well as our own expectations from ourselves.

Expectations are key factors that drive our behavior...

Whatever you choose to do in life will have an impact on the future expectations of others (your environmental expectations). ***Whether you demonstrate success or failure the expectations of others will adjust to reinforce that behavior...***

***

Your environmental expectations will adapt as you modify your own behavior.

***

To tie this all together, what I would like you to consider is the possible relationship between the general concept of the Observer Effect as it relates to our earlier discussion of the Placebo Effect.

The Placebo Effect is caused by the <u>*expected*</u> observation of changes. I suggest that the Placebo Effect is a special case of the Observer Effect.

As we saw with the Placebo Effect the 'observer' could have been the test patient or the scientist, depending on which one knows who has the test medicine. We know that if either one knows (i.e. observes) who has the real medicine then the outcome of the test is altered due to **expectations alone...**

How does this help us? Remember that we said people will seek better information regarding the elements that drive events toward the future? The very process of observing and understanding the direction of change introduces a new observer into the equation. **This new observer is YOU.**

***

<u>*This*</u> *is how you can define your own Destiny:*

The process of observing (i.e. visualizing, expecting) your desired outcome will 'collapse' and 'resolve' the specific potentialities that actualize into your chosen future.

***

This conclusion will be confirmed by your own experiences. For now I ask you to please just consider and reflect on the above statement… If there is any truth to be found it is here...

Remember, to expect something means that you <u>believe</u> it can actually happen.

This gets us close to an 'integration' of the concepts in this discussion…

We continually alter reality with our expectations. This happens whether we are aware of it or not.

So the real question becomes: What do you *expect* to happen in the future?

***

Persistent expectation of a given future is the 'catalyst' for that future...

<u>This is Lesson Number 3</u>

***

In other words, simply:

***

Make a *meaningful* decision:

This will push the right triggers...

And **this** WILL cut the right strings...

***

So what does it really mean to create your own Destiny?

Behave as you *have behaved* and nothing changes...

34

The key to directing the course of your Destiny is to behave in a way that is **unexpected...**

You will not be granted a Destiny unless you are willing to break free from the negative influences that exist in your life.

Fate makes us react as we do. This means is that our behavior is always 'understandable' for each of us simply because of who we are. Behavior is always understandable on hindsight, given the environmental influences that surround us, our childhood traumas, and of course our *state of mind* at the time of the event...

It is when people 'rise above' their own constraints in life that we applaud them.

Think about it.

Unexpected behavior is the <u>*process*</u> that allows you to break free from the endless and self-fulfilling relationship between you and your environment...

Unexpected behavior *distinguishes* Fate from Destiny.

***

So HOW do I do this? How can the Observer Effect change my life? What exactly am I supposed to do differently than what I'm already doing?

It is simple: Abandon the subjective constraints of 'Reality' and expect to achieve <u>*what you really want instead*</u>. Anyone can behave as expected... *It is your remarkable new behavior that causes Reality to <u>adjust its expectations of</u> YOU.*

***

Improving the expectations for your future is what it *means* to create your own Destiny. This is the ongoing process itself...

***

If you understand this then you will also see why it was so important to explain how and why to <u>manage</u> your anxiety levels... You now have the simple secret to achieving **whatever** you want… and the better you are able to grasp this the more overwhelming it can be…

***

"Give me a lever long enough and a fulcrum on which to place it, and I shall move the world."[*]

***

---

[*] Archimedes

A Brief Timeout...

Hopefully, the last few pages have made an impact on your perceptions...

It was necessary to go through the first chapters and lessons in order to express the importance and simple truth of how your expectations (and those of others) change the world...

If you don't yet understand <u>*why and how*</u> you <u>*must*</u> 'see your future' with clarity and confidence then you should probably go back to the very beginning of this discussion and start over. You haven't seen the big picture yet... Every concept in this discussion is there for a specific purpose.

If you don't know that Lesson Number 3 is a statement of fact, then you will derive little benefit from this entire discussion.

(One hint... it involves faith. See Chapter 1; Making Decisions)

***

"That a man can change himself... and master his own destiny is the conclusion of every [right] mind..."*

***

---

*Christian D. Larson, paraphrased

3) Cause and Effect:

The Truth about the Power of Choice

1: What Do You Want?

As we discussed earlier, there is at any time an infinite number of potentialities that exist in your future. You can, with Lesson Number 3, choose to 'observe and collapse' any one of them to make it become REAL.

This is actually the easier part. The harder part is to choose which future you actually want…

***

If you don't know what you want then you are not going to get it

***

Fortunately there is a rational approach to answering this difficult but required question. Micro-Economics explains this problem in terms of 'Opportunity Costs'.

Micro-Economics tells us that when we choose a specific path we are in fact foregoing, or giving up, all the other paths that we *could have chosen*. A simple example might be a desire to live on a tropical island. Let's say you choose to live in Tahiti. If you do so, then you are foregoing (giving up) the opportunity of living in Hawaii, or any other suitable location (at least at the same time).

Another issue that we should consider is that once you commit to a certain future, you are responsible for all aspects of that decision. This includes any undesirable consequences that you may not have foreseen.

Further, because you can direct your own destiny, you might find it beneficial to simply create an environment that will generally make you happy, instead of striving for a specific measurable goal.

Icarus created a quote that addresses these issues and more. It is disarmingly simple, but it encompasses the essence of what you should do with your ability to stand your ground and *maintain your **own** expectations*...

***

"Create the conditions that you desire"

This is Icarus's Lesson 4

***

This particular statement best *summarizes the essence of this Philosophy*: Yes, you can re-establish and re-enforce your priorities and behaviors with visualization: But you can also **intentionally manipulate environmental factors** *to reinforce your desired **behavior***...

This is the power of the observer (You) to create the path that leads you to **behave in the way** that creates your desired 'results'. What environmental factors would encourage **you** to be happy and effective? Create *those conditions*...

This allows you to 'redirect' yourself towards your desires, as we have discussed, but also to be 'pulled' forward by the environmental influences that 'expect' and encourage you to succeed...

If you are concerned that reaching a specific goal would require lots of stress and effort, why not create an environment that would enable you to achieve this goal with no effort at all? Perhaps an environment that makes the process fun.

***

You can alter your environmental influences to influence, in turn, your own desired behavior. You can be 'drawn' towards your own chosen Destiny...

***

Altering your environmental influences can be very simple. You can use this process as a 'first step' towards shaping your Destiny. Start with something small...

Example: do you have a favorite place in your home? What simple things could you do to make it an even better place for you? (i.e. what are some desirable potentialities?) A new lamp? A throw rug? Perhaps you could take the ten minutes it would require to clean and dust your favorite spot.

Perhaps you could move your furniture around... Choose a simple step that is easy to do.

Once you have made such a change, carefully notice what you have achieved in relation to this discussion. By improving your favorite spot you have:

1) *Observed and collapsed a **potentiality***
2) Altered your environmental influences
3) Therefore altered your destiny in a desirable way

True, we do such small tasks all the time… the point is that now you can coordinate your efforts with a sense of *purpose*…

Who can deny the ancient wisdom of the Japanese people to enhance their homes: In order to provide the maximum sense of harmony and quiet focus? They have made an 'Art Form' of 'creating desirable conditions', in order to achieve a **desired state of mind…**

Alertness without anxiety

This same wisdom can be applied to all aspects of your life.

The clarity and strength of your **desires** will <u>proportionately coordinate</u> your **efforts** so that you become truly 'invested in your own destiny'.

All you have to do is decide what you really want… and clearly visualize it happening until you know that somehow **it will happen,** and you will *'fracture' the weaknesses in Reality to bring your desired potentialities into existence…*

This is the 'net effect' of the application of this philosophy

Decide what you want, and treat every small step as a meaningful step towards a much larger life… Full of reward and free from anxiety…

***

Lesson 4 is also important because there is an apparent contradiction in two statements we have discussed: on the one hand we said that no-one could ever predict the future absolutely, yet we are saying that you can create your own future by simply observing a desired potentiality…

It should never be assumed that any specific aspects of your desires will occur exactly as you expect: *Expect to be surprised...*

There may be legitimate reasons for you to want to modify your goals. You can change your future literally as easily as you can change your mind... This in no way equates to failure, unless you have told others and have publicly committed to a specific goal. In this case you may feel pressure to keep rigid goals that don't allow for the give and take of any environmental changes, including the existence of other people's desires. You may be required to do this at your work environment, but remember not to talk about your personal goals to anyone except your very most trusted...

This leads us to the concept of empathy. There are people in this world who have absolutely no sense of empathy towards others. This means that they can not or will not view issues from other people's points of view. Theirs is the only point of view that matters. We have all met such people and I expect you will agree that there is very little to like or respect about them.

You will create fewer confrontations if you maintain a sense of empathy towards others. Take the realtiy of other people's desires as environmental factors for you to work *within*... (i.e. Lesson 1, page 13)

***

Be flexible enough with your own goals so that you can accommodate changes in your environment as well as the desires of others.

This is Icarus's Lesson Number 5

***

2: Oxymoron: Meaningful Coincidence

An oxymoron is a label that is applied to phrases that contain self-contradictory meanings. These are usually fun to play with because they can reveal apparent paradoxes.

The phrase 'deafening silence' is a good example of an oxymoron. Another is 'soft edges'.

The term 'meaningful coincidence' is also an oxymoron, but it is far more than just fun with words. This term is associated more with philosophy than science and is a rich and fascinating topic for our discussion.

A Meaningful Coincidence refers to two or more events that seem extremely (even astronomically) unlikely, yet combine to provide specific meaning to you.

A good example might be something you forgot about years ago, yet re-emerges at just the right time to help you when you really need it.

You will recognize it when it happens. Such events will cause you to 'thank your stars' for your 'luck' or to be otherwise astonished.

It is a type of 'everyday miracle' that I am describing.

One way to know that you are faced with such a miracle is that it will always be far more meaningful to you as an individual than it will to someone else. In other words, you and you alone will know that it is not a mere coincidence. Generally, it's probably not wise to even try to explain these special events to others. Other people will find it much easier to believe that it is just a 'lucky break'.

Let them believe what they want. It is your experience that matters here…

The reason that this is an important topic to our discussion is that as your level of skill with this philosophy rises you will start to have more and more of these meaningful events.

This can be both intimidating and scary if you are not prepared for it. You may feel a sense of the 'unreal' as doors are suddenly opened for you.

You may feel that something else is manipulating events, or that things are suddenly 'far too easy'. The simple truth will be that you have learned to dynamically alter reality, and you are directly witnessing the results. This fact is little understood because there are not many people who have learned how to do this yet...

And those who do know are the 'movers and shakers' of this world.

The way we should receive these events should be as rewards for our efforts, however we choose to define them. Meaningful coincidences confirm that we are on the right path to our chosen future. These are special 'previews' on the patterns that we are 'carving' into reality. They may contain warnings, and such warnings need to be incorporated into our plans...but even a warning is a helpful message.

Conclusion

What we perceive to be Reality, through our subjective and supposedly rational viewpoints, is in fact riddled with irrational components. These are the 'weaknesses' and 'patterns' in the fabric of reality that we have been discussing.

A tornado is not exactly 'rational'.

Chaos is not rational.

There is the possibility that your Boss, or a loved one, will not be rational.

Any of these could devastate your life...

This perspective runs counter to Western style thinking... Reality, in fact, is hard wired with unpredictable and complex patterns, ripples, and feedback loops. Many of these emanate from the *mind of man*. We see such patterns whenever people interact.

Only the **mind** can explain the Placebo Effect or the Observer Effect.

And what if we actually dared **use** these proven phenomena?

As 'The Observer' of your own life you can use the Observer Effect... The process of (intensely) visualizing what you want and believing it can happen will cause uncounted probabilities to collapse... Unless something unexpected gets in the way...

Yet the future remains full of infinite possibilities...

So there you have it: A simple and self-perpetuating way of living life to its fullest... You can become your own 'force of nature'. Your *'mind's eye'* is the ***tool that alters the real...***

We impose Order on the Chaos of Nature. This is Mankind's Destiny...

It is so simple but it is **not easy to do**... Why?

Anxiety can create an unreasoning hesitation when you begin implementing this process. As we have learned this is simple fear... and fear is not rational.

Whenever you get stuck just disengage by focusing on the NOW and visualize ways to change something in your *environment*: Something that you can at least have an influence on... Turn on some music! ...Set aside some quiet time. Visualize yourself *without* anxiety.

This will in turn have a positive effect on you.

The rest is just following the steps that will be provided to you. These steps will be the result of visualizing <u>what you want</u>. Yes, you must see it very clearly before you can make it real, but as always the most important thing is that you must *believe it can actually happen*...

This does not imply that you will achieve your dreams in a few simple steps: The real challenge will be the issue of *maintaining* your vision throughout the storms of your life.

Your life, and the way that you choose to live it, is the only reality you will ever experience in this world.

In the final analysis, the way that you choose to live is the ultimate expression of how you value life's precious gift: *and time is limited*... Time is the only real thing that any of us really have...

So trade the precious time and energy that you are wasting with worry and guilt for time dedicated to thinking about what you really want. This is the simple path to Self-Actualization...

There is one last lesson of caution, depending on the scope of your desires. For example, if you desire to be the next Napoleon or Alexander the Great:

"I dare do all that may become a man; Who dares do more is none."*

In today's words,

I will dare to do anything that reflects my limits as a human being: Anyone who dares to do more will be destroyed by the results.

You are only human...

But being human places you among the most amazing creations in the universe...

Invest Yourself in Your Destiny
Create the Conditions that You Desire

***

"Believe and you will find your way"**

---

*Macbeth, Act I, Sc. VII
** "May It Be" by Roma Ryan

To achieve Self-Actualization, simply understand that...

A: You are an active player in your own future whether you believe it or not

B: Decisions direct behavior and behavior affects Reality

Your decisions directly alter your Future

Have you decided what you **really want** out of Life?

If you have, then your decisions will be shielded from negative influences while expanding upon the opportunities that are presented to you

Your behavior automatically synchronizes with behavior that is consistent with the achievement of what you really want to have **happen**...

You become the person that you want to be

Your entire life reflects the harmony and happiness that **YOU** have **decided** it to be

***

"The seasons are passing one by one…

*So gather moments while you may,
Collect the dreams you dream today"*[*]

***

---

[*] Paul Anka, "The Times of Your Life"

References

1) Solomon, Robert C. (1987). From Hegel to Existentialism. Oxford University Press. pp. 238. ISBN 0195061829. [http://books.google.com/books?id=3JA3vyj4slsC&pg=PA238].

2) Robert C. Solomon, Existentialism (McGraw-Hill, 1974, pages 1–2)

3) D.E. Cooper Existentialism: A Reconstruction (Basil Blackwell, 1999, page 8)

4,5,6) Unknown Author, "Existentialism" [http://en.wikipedia.org/wiki/Existentialism] 8/1/09

www.ingramcontent.com/pod-product-compliance
Lightning Source LLC
Chambersburg PA
CBHW060354050426
42449CB00011B/2983